GenerationX

Lesson's in life

By Amanda Jervis

You can obtain permission by e-mail:
GenerationXlessinlife@hotmail.co.uk

Distributed by Lulu.com

Available at www.lulu.com

ISBN: 978-0-9556767-0-3

Contents:

Dear Reader,

Welcome to my first collection of poems. After being published in 25 different books I thought it was about time I brought out a book of my own. I've had a lot of adversity through my life. That I have managed to overcome to the best of my ability, these experiences good and bad have inspired me, helped me grow into the person I have become. (Even if I'm a little bit neurotic!)
I would like to give a special thanks to my friends Amber and Charlie, Ollie and Sarah, Jason and Kate, Nathan and Natalie, Andy and Michele, Jade, Jay, Kimmie, Sam and Debz who have been there for me and helped me through some very difficult times.
To my friend Ashley, who dreamed up the title and designed the cover of this book and my family, especially my Mum, whom I love.
Well I suppose I should stop going on and let you read the book. I hope you enjoy it.

A. Jervis
X

I dedicate this book to my son Anton
And to the memory of my children
Jenna and Lewis

Bully Boy

Power to do what ever he'd choose,
I'm just a bully boy's toy,
His pride and joy,
To use and abuse,
On his quest to own my soul,
Thirsting for power to be in control,
Only satisfied when he'd reached his goal,
But I opened my eyes to reveal the truth behind
his disguise,
I was naive to believe we could reach great
heights,
As I could not see the chemistry,
Was to be an explosion of possessive aggression,
He kept pulling me apart bit by bit,
Making me weaker wanting to die,
I'm glad I realised why,
He may not know it but he made me strong,
To fight away the control he'd already won.

Fabric of society

The moral fabric of society is decaying,
The politicians keep on praying,
"Is there no way of saving this land we hold so dear?"
We have toddlers drinking beer,
Teenagers smoking gear,
Sexual perversion becoming the norm,
Ripping through society like a storm,
A tornado, a hurricane,
That causes so much pain,
The only future I can see,
Is one of greed and of money,
With no respect for themselves or others,
People who rape their own mothers!
A deep set evil has corrupted us all,
Here to make the human race fall,
Gun crazed posse roam the street,
Killing youngsters for the shoes on their feet,
Shooting others for the most pettiest things,
All caught up in this gangster ting,
No care or respect for anothers life,
They slash at anyone with a knife,
They would even stab their wife!
So much hatred has hardened our hearts,
There's no more love or compassion,
There's no more security.
Sounds like hell on earth to me.
Its time for us to open our hearts,
Call to God once more,
Who can help us all restore,
The peace and harmony we search for,
Because there is so much selfishness in this place,
We're going to end up destroying our race,
We're becoming extinct, like the dinosaurs before,
The frail human race will be no more.

Nature, In Abuse

A physical manifestation,
Of an emotional state,
Cutting themselves all over the place,
It's like a new style of tattoo,
That's going around like the flu,
An epidemic destroying our youth,
Why are they filled with so much hate?
Or is it just anger they cannot dissipate,
They cause themselves pain to release the emotional
strains,
Of pent up frustration caused by societies expectations,
Surely there's another way to deal with the pressures of
life,
There's got to be a better way than cutting with a knife,
The shame and embarrassment they will endure,
When it comes to explaining what the scars are for,
What will they do? What will they say?
Because they know it will happen one day,
Why don't they go for a run instead?
It's better than slashing their arms and legs,
Leaving scars that remain forever,
It's not clever!
They cut themselves deeper and deeper each time,
Trying to get the same high, from the intense sensation,
That rushes through their bodies,
What they need is some kind of hobby,
That will take them away from the eternal hate,
That's stolen their desire to be great,
And made them think their life is shit,
Willing to do the dying bit,

They punish themselves every day,
For all the things they could not say,
Riddled with guilt for the thoughts that they had,
Their own minds slowly driving them mad,
Confused and tormented by the things that they do,
Blinded from finding anything new,
That will help them cope from day to day,
With all the things that life throws their way,
They do not realize or identify,
The negative emotion they feel inside,
Is the same as everyone who's alive!

Sunshine rays

On a cloudy day,
I look to the sky,
And watch as some clouds move on by,
I start to cry,
As memories of my childhood,
Flood my mind,
When the rays of sunshine,
Catch my eyes,
Streaming to earth from the sky,
I remember my beliefs,
That have now long died,
Of when I thought they were God,
Collecting lost souls,
To take up them up to his heavenly abode,
But now I am older,
With knowledge acquired,
I now know it's only the sun,
That shines lines in the sky,
It's not Gods guiding light,
But still the truth I have discovered,
From deep within my soul,
It something that I feel,
God is definitely real.

Finding God

Many men try to find God,
By looking with their eyes,
And judging with their minds,
They will not accept,
What they're trying to find,
Is waiting deep inside,
When they wake up,
And take a look inside,
They will be surprised,
For all the knowledge,
That they need to know,
Is locked away within their soul,
When they change their attitude,
And learn to control their mind,
The truth is never hard to find,
God has been with them since the start of time,
It's only the illusion of the mind,
That causes many people to be blind,
And lose their way on their destined line.

<u>Storm</u>

Sitting outside on a warm summers night,

Suddenly the sky is filled with a flash of light,

As I draw in a breath,

My nostrils flare,

As I smell the static in the air,

A clap of thunder echoes in the sky,

The force of nature is all around,

Making loud banging sounds,

The awesome power the storm possesses,

Makes me feel like I'm nothing at all,

As when Mother Nature calls,

She can make us all fall.

Suffragette

This is for the suffragettes,
Who suffered in the past,
To change the course of history,
To give women the chance,
To prove themselves worthy,
Of being equal to man,
They had to act like savages,
To fulfill their plan,
They broke windows in Downing Street,
By throwing little stones,
"We have to stop them!"
The politicians moaned,
They tried to storm the House of Commons,
But to no avail,
It just got 24 of them,
Thrown into jail,
Many of them refused to eat,
Becoming very ill,
Prisons did not want martyrs,
So they were force fed against their will,
The politicians were frantic,
So they brought in a new bill,
Nicknamed the "cat and mouse act" to do their will,
They'd released the poor women from their torturous
hell,
Then re-arrest them when again well,
The suffragettes continued with their campaign,
Setting fire to private and public property the same,
It wasn't until war broke out,
In the Eastern Europe domain,

That the government saw,
They would be needing women more,
When all the men got drafted into war,
But the women still had to protest,
For a change in the law,
Even after their efforts during war,
It wasn't until 1918,
That a reprieve was seen,
When women of thirty could vote,
So when it comes to the next election,
Women please do remember,
If it wasn't for the suffragettes
You would still be classed,
As the second class gender!

Talent with in us all

Why are we so blind to see?

What is created in eachothers company,

From appreciation emerged inspiration,

Awakened from its dormant state,

A talent so great, a pleasure to hear,

Why hide such a gift because somebody sneers?

Do not be ignorant of the gift that you hold,

That given a chance can help others indulge,

In a spiritual high, giving them the strength to achieve,

In learning life's lessons, that will keep them safe,

Until the time comes when their life force goes,

Leaving behind this mortal place,

To transcend upon the astral plane,

To learn new lessons of a new age,

As their souls travel on, through to the next stage.

Buskers song

I wish I could hold a talent so bold,

Like the wondering soul of a busker,

Who has no job to hold him down,

From singing the songs that were lost and now found,

As we've gone on our mission, to mix in societies condition

He hasn't gone mad with another mans plan,

He is living his life as calm as he can,

Not losing himself in societies plan,

To me he seems a happy man,

Free to wonder around this land,

With the clothes that he wears,

And the dreads in his hair,

Lots of people stop and stare,

But they do not see him standing there,

They see what they want, but he doesn't care,

For he knows it is them that is going nowhere.

Six kids

I thought I could cope,
I thought I'd be all right,
With all these kids,
For a couple of nights,
How wrong I was,
I have to admit,
With their fighting, squabbling and crying,
It felt like I was dying,
With all this noise around,
I could not cope,
I wanted some help,
But no one was there,
Some people came round,
But they soon disappeared,
It must be all this noise,
They could hear!

Moment in time

When I look deep into your eyes,

I have a strange feeling that's supreme and divine,

If only I could spend just one moment in time,

Holding you close, as if you were mine,

My hopes and dreams become one entwined,

Memories of this moment forever be mine,

For me to enjoy time after time,

Longing for the day, when you're finally mine,

So we can spend, just a moment in time,

To make our lives entwined.

Song of the sea

As I listen to the crashing of the waves,
And the rustling of the stones,
I go into a trance with their mesmerizing tones,
All I can hear is the song of the sea,
It's like it's calling me,
Come in, come in and then you'll be free,
As the waves leave the shore,
It's pulling me in more,
Into the sea where I might be free,
From this sweltering heat on this sunny day,
That has cost me more than I wanted to pay,
I feel like I'm ready to die,
Then a child knocks me as he runs by,
The mesmerizing spell is broken,
The sea will have to wait for another day,
Before it can take my life away!

Drugs mission

It starts with a smoke,
They call it dope,
Then with an E now and then,
But I'm still not one of them,
It don't matter to me,
What I use is clean,
I ain't a dirty junkie,
With their clothes and skin that hum and a din,
I am clean now I'm on my amphetamine,
Next stop I.V.
But it don't matter to me,
For I am still clean,
Even though I I.V. amphetamine,
I would never I.V. that heroin,
Or I'd soon become a hum and a din,
I will have a toot now and then,
But I will never be buying,
That's what I thought,
But I must have been lying,
Now I am a junkie,
With clothes and skin that hum and a din,
This bed I'm now in,
Is where I'm dying.

I accept

As I look back in time,
I sometimes regret you're not mine,
For the years we were together,
I had hoped our love would be strong,
Until them three days where it went badly
wrong,
When I got hurt for something we'd both done,
I had an affair because he showed me he cared,
You had your affairs because they were bare,
You punched me and kicked me,
Then told me you cared,
I begged you for mercy,
But it fell on deaf ears,
As you kept on punching me through my tears,
Our time had now passed by,
Our dreams lay broken in our weeping eyes,
Our hopes of a love so great,
Faded away and died.

Deep in regret

Reality is on a time road,

Man, Woman, White or Black,

It doesn't matter where you're at,

Just as long as you know there's no turning
back,

Some souls forget that they need to
accept,

That the past has gone by,

Whether a nightmare or a dream,

It's just a flickering screen,

A show in your mind, to consume your time,

Into the guilt, the misery or the fun times,

To remind you of the things you left
behind,

The future it seems,

Lives in fantasy realms,

Where our dreams and hopes can be found,

Where life can be what you want it to be,

Full of total happiness and glee,

But I am full of misery,

Nothing in life seems good to me,

Hung up on the past, that's what's happened
to me,

Twisted and bitter,

From my screen that flickers,

Night and day I see the pictures,

Of the chances I've missed of having pure
bliss,

Because of my ignorance and fear,

Now I sit here in my twilight years,

I look back in tears,

For the future for me is looking bleak,

And my past is full of darkness,

That's overwhelmed my present day,

But I suppose it's the price I have to pay,

For choosing to waste my life away!

<u>Feeling small</u>

It's obvious to see, so my friends tell me,

That you don't fancy me at all,

Well I'm sorry I make your skin crawl,

Do you think I like being known as a fool?

With everyone laughing and joking at my expense,

Ridiculing me and making me tense,

Right now, death to me makes sense,

How can you enjoy making another person feel so small?

You can't be human after all.

Lost love

The light which shone from within your eyes,

Seems to have faded away and died,

Can you tell me why?

It was not me that told the lies,

The words I spoke were true,

Couldn't you see the love I had for you?

A love that could have been so true,

Has now faded away and turned blue.

Lesson of control

In the darkest years,
Of my recent past,
Nothing ever seemed to last,
I'd control others for self-gain,
I'd give them love and then I'd give them pain,
But I never injured or maimed.

I'd play them silly head games,
To make them insecure,
So they would panic if I walked out the door,
Frightened of what could be in store,
Without me to hold their hand,
It was something I couldn't understand,
To be controlled by another man,
Until it happened to me!

I was so ignorant, I could not see,
What it was, he was doing to me,
He taken control of my mind and my body,
But he never got hold of my soul,
Which came shining through at the near end,
To give me the power to be me again!

Now I see the lesson,
I chose to learn from it,
So I never get controlled again,
As next time there will be more pain,
As things are never quite the same...

Darkest moments

In my darkest moments of sorrow and
despair,
I kept on calling but no one was there,
Then someone tells me of a great man,
Who comes from another land,
And who holds the key to life itself,
The knowledge,
This gave me inspiration to change my life,
Start doing what I know is right,
From that day, I became enlightened,
I was no longer frightened,
For I knew you were there,
Although I did not see you,
I knew I was under your care,
Sometimes I'd think I was mad,
When others told me so,
But this much I do know,
My life is more complete,
Now I believe,
I may be mad,
But I'm happy not sad.

A cry for help

On the outside I look strong,

But on the inside I am weak,

I look as if I'm happy,

But inside I'm crying,

Sometimes it feels like I'm dying,

I feel so alone,

I feel so scared,

I feel unloved,

Why do I feel this way?

I'm trying to escape,

But I can't get out,

It feels like I'm going crazy,

With no one to help,

Help, help, help!

No one hears,

So I will keep on hiding behind my tears,

For many years.

Destinies time

I know it's not hard to see,

There's something that you do to me,

It's a feeling deep inside,

It happens every time you're by my side,

It's a feeling I haven't had for some time,

And because of this, I wish I could read your mind,

So I can see if you have that feeling deep inside for me,

The one that keeps saying "make up your mind"

Or your might find,

Destinies time passes you by,

Because there will never be another try,

Believe me its true,

Now would I lie to you?

You're being watched

No matter what you think,

No matter what you do,

There is always someone watching you,

You must be good to succeed,

Don't let your life be run by greed,

Many people take this path,

And although they have all they need,

They can never be happy with their greed,

They can never be satisfied,

With what they've got,

Because of greed, they want the lot.

Beer goggles

You slime up to a girl and turn on the charm,
Buy her a drink and lead her by the arm,
To a cosy, quiet corner of the pub,
So you can huddle up and chat,
Hiding in the corner black,
You lie through your teeth,
To get back to her flat,
A night of passion with a total stranger,
Don't know her name or the age of her!
But when the harsh light of day,
Shines upon the face at your side lays,
Age you could not last night see,
Because of your juvenility,
Blinded by booze as you have done before,
You start heading for the door,
Praying that she doesn't wake up,
You don't want a messy break up!

<u>Secret</u>

Lord hear my cry,
I didn't want to lie,
I was told a secret,
To take to my death,
Or it would create a mess,
I wish I could have cleared my conscience sooner,
But it would have ruined her,
Like a cancer it's been eating me away,
But I promised I would never say,
Until the end of my mortal days,
Now that time has come,
The secret must be sung,
I cannot go to my grave,
Till my soul is saved,
I must confess all I know,
Divulge the truth that I do hold,
I need to be bold,
To release the paradox of old,
For 40 years I've lied and deceived,
All because of someone's greed,
I covered the truth, buried it deep,
Even trampled it under my feet,
But now the time has come,
For the mistakes of the past to be undone,
Forgive me lord I do pray,
For the truth I now do say,
To save my soul I have to tell,
To stop me spiralling down to hell!

<u>What right do we have to judge another?</u>

We're all part of the human race,
Plodding along at our own pace,
Each learning the lessons to be taught,
So don't become lost or distraught.

Each lessons comes with experience,
But it's up to you at what expense,
You allow yourself to be judged,
So don't continue with a grudge.

Though no-one has the right to say,
You live your life, in your own way,
But don't force yourself upon another,
Treat as though he is your brother.

Don't steal, Insult, attack, degrade,
Trust what is right and you'll be repaid,
Look inside and search for your light,
Choose the path you <u>know</u> is right.

It is not for us to judge your move,
But it's up to you, if you want to improve,
Lessons come with the life you lead,
You'll get what you're owed, it's guaranteed!
Bear this in mind and you may discover,
What right have we to judge another?

No need to be aggressive

I don't like your attitude to life,

Why can't you just be nice?

There is no need to be aggressive,

Every time things stop progressing,

The way you expected them to go,

Because as destinies time takes its toll,

Things may go fast, they may go slow,

So don't let your emotions overflow,

And never lose control.

Bubble machine

I'm staring into the abyss,

Of a bubble machine,

Where every bubble has captured a dream,

That goes floating off into space,

Heading for the human race,

Where every dream has a place,

Deep within the minds,

Of the sleeping mankind,

Good ones, bad ones, lustful, not

Every one has got a slot.

Doubt

Oh my lord, I need your help,

To release me from this doubt,

That has blurred my vision of what's right,

To help to enhance my life,

For you know my soul, inside and out,

So you know about this doubt,

I try and try with all my heart,

To commit from the start,

But due to doubt,

Of what could be,

Am I due to fail consistently?

Mission of love

Being in love with someone,

Can bring many wondrous things,

The days seem brighter,

Whenever the birds start to sing,

The glow of the sun,

Enhances the warmth in my heart,

As I think of the mission,

I'm about to start,

From when I first saw you,

I knew it was you,

That could bring me a love,

That will make all my dreams,

Come true.

Ignorance is bliss

They say ignorance is bliss,
But I think it just makes it easier,
For people to take the piss,
Living a life with no consequence,
No guilt or regret for the things you've done,
The stealing, the lying, people dying,
Watching over your shoulder,
For someone with a gun,
Living your life on the run,
Live by the sword, die by the sword,
Takes many a young life away,
When will they realise,
That's not the way to play,
They may think their life is better than others,
That others lives are just a bore,
But one day they may discover,
A life of peace and harmony,
Has many rewards.

Connection deep inside

When destiny directed our paths to collide,

There was a connection deep inside,

Letting us know which way to go,

To gain more knowledge for our souls,

How long it will last I do not know?

As this is something I have never known,

A relationship where I'm not being controlled,

I didn't want someone spoiling my fun,

Trying to tell me how my life should be run,

I was waiting for someone right to come,

Who would not judge me,

On the things I've done,

Who will love me for me,

And not what I could be.

Neurotic fool

I'm just a neurotic fool,

But is it any wonder,

With what I've been through?

Life's little trials got a bit too much,

And I always thought I was tough!

But as I sit in my cell of self pity,

Closing myself off more and more,

Chained down by memories of despair,

As past comes to haunt me once more,

I only wish I could close the door,

So the wounds do not feel so raw.

Let go of fear

So many attitudes are ruled by fear,
It stops the truth from coming near,
To give you the strength to be you,
But it is easy to do,
To get the truth to come to you,
It has to be induced from deep inside,
Not by joining a church nearby,
Living in hope and looking at the sky,
Waiting in fear for the days to pass by,
Waiting for the day that you die,
Life is for living; you're here to enjoy,
Look at natures little toys,
For the beauty that they hold,
That can help release your soul,
So let go of fear and the grip that it holds,
Start following life day by day,
With no expectations of what should be,
Cause it can't be wrong, when you're feeling ok.

Waiting for the reaper to come

The fires of hell keep on burning,
As my cycle of life keeps on turning,
Consuming my life one day at a time,
Until it comes to the last of the line,
When my body is frail and my mind forgetful,
When I can no longer stand,
Fingers curled up by chronic arthritis,
Hands can no longer help me dress,
People wonder why I'm depressed,
My life is over,
It will soon be the end,
Just waiting for the reaper to come,
Then my life on this earth will be done.

True friend

You are my true friend,

As far as I'm concerned,

I will always be here for you,

As we go through this life,

Learning the lessons to be learned,

You can always count on my friendship,

For as long as we both shall live,

I will always be honest and true to you,

And I hope you'll be the same way too,

As lovers may come and go,

But to you my friend I will always show,

Love and understanding in whichever path you take,

And as long as you always remember,

I will love you my friend,

Even with the mistakes.

Meditation

In the noisy confusion of my mind,
I keep on trying to find,
Some way out of this spoiled place,
That's consumed by greed,
With mans ever-increasing need,
To be bigger and better than before,
Owing more and more,
But as I settle for my quietude,
My mind starts telling me lies,
Telling me the place I search for,
This peace of mind I'm trying to find,
Is only a dream,
That lives within imaginary realms,
And it can never be found,
But I persevere in my search,
To find the silence of my mind,
The noisy confusion started to dim,
And a light started shining deep within,
A feeling of peace and contentment
Rushed through my soul,
And I knew I had found my goal.

Despair

When there is nothing left except sorrow and despair,

When you cry out for help but no one is there,

When you've reach the end of a bottomless pit,

When you're wishing for a grave marked R.I.P.

When you've tried and tried to loosen the grip,

From all these things that drain you drip by drip,

That keeps making you ill and making you sick,

Do you want to do the dying bit?

Turn to God for the peace that you search for,

And let the negative energy be dispelled,

That can send your life spiralling downwards,

Into a painful, torturous hell.

Please listen to what I have to say,

That will help you and other people one-day,

To bring them out of darkness and decay,

Into the light of Gods brilliant rays.

GenerationX

Things of youth get left behind,

As we mature from our childlike minds,

Thoughts get cluttered with our daily chores,

The modern society flaws,

It steals our sight,

Of what's wrong and what's right,

As society becomes complacent,

24-7 people we've become,

Rushing around with lots to be done,

No time for relaxation, no time for fun,

Just lots and lots of work to come,

No one to tend to our children's moral needs,

No one planting the right seeds,

Of honour and trust, Generosity not greed,

It's something our society needs,

Because it's decaying more and more,

Who knows what's next to be in store,

We're destroying ourselves on a daily basis,

Polluting our rivers and seas,

Cutting down all of the trees,

That are there to help us breathe,

Society blinded from what's going on,

By a consumer greed,

We always want more than we need,

No aspiration, No dreams to fulfill,

Just a living a life paying credit card bills.

Death

Death is the only thing guaranteed in this life,
So why when it happens,
Does it create so much strife?
It upsets us so much,
It cuts like a knife,
Crying all the time,
You just want to hide.

As time goes by, depression sets in,
To lock your mind in, its negative spin,
It can feel like there is no way to win,
No way of stopping your life becoming dim,
The future is looking grim.

For you, its seems, there is no light,
It makes you want to give up the fight,
Because nothing in your life is going right,
You don't know where to go,
You don't know what to do,
Everything in life seems lost to you.

But a friend comes by, to let you know,
That you are not doing this alone,
No matter how bad you feel,
You have a friend who's real,
Who will stand by your side,
And help you through this stage of life.

Blood Test

What's wrong with the men today?
Loads of blokes just want to play,
Having sex with no matter who,
Planting their seed wherever they go,
But never staying around to watch their children grow,
Dipping their dicks in as many girls as they can,
Do they want to catch everything - is that the plan?
With Syphilis, Hepatitis, H.I.V. and Aids,
There's a lot of disease about nowadays,
That without a blood test you would never know,
As there are no tell tell signs, nothing to show,
So how would you know...
If the last girl you slept with, was infected bro?
Without a condom you're playing a game of Russian roulette,
Surely life's too precious to be used as a bet,
Maybe you're contaminating every girl that you meet,
Poisoning their blood from their head to their feet,
Then they will go on spreading the rotten germs,
Polluting the gene pool - Will they ever learn?
So do not be ignorant,
And condemn someone to death,
Be a man, and go have the test.

Vigilante

The wheels spin round
The brakes did stop
The hand that shows me what you've got
The hand that makes the traffic stop
The children cross the road
The man that holds the lollipop
Pop pop the gun did shot
Shot the man who holds the rocks
The children scream
The wheels did screech
No brakes to stop
Gunman running from the cops
Dead man lying on road to rot
Rotting flesh of wretched man
People watch and stand
Police do ask "who is this?"
People shout "don't take the piss,
He be selling crack to our kids"
No law to protect
Vengeance assigned
Retribution done by a single guy

Dark, lonely place

My life was a dark lonely place,
Full of despair, hate and disgrace,
I'd wake up each morning,
Wishing I was dead,
To stop the hurting in my head,
From all the disappointments I've had in my life,
People letting me down, giving me strife,
Then someone opened me a door,
That could give me happiness and so much more,
At first I though it was a load of bull,
But now I think its cool,
Jesus has opened a special place,
Far away from the rat race,
That's been decaying my mind over time,
Making me think I'm going insane,
Lost in the confusion of emotional pain,
That I have suffered with since the day I was born,
I kept hoping it would pass like a storm,
When the darkness has gone and the sun shines once
more,
And everything is restored as before,
I'm waiting for my time to come,
When all the healing of the past is done!

No Good for You

Twisted perversion of a love gone wrong,
No sweet words of a love song,
Just pain and hurt that comes along,
With everyday that passes.

You must question yourself everyday,
To how it has come to be this way,
With nothing in common, nothing at all,
So why in love were you to fall?

Were you blinded by emotion?
Deprived of perception, deprived of sense,
Are you truly that dense?
Could you not see?
What this man was doing to thee?

He messes you up with mind games,
To make you insecure,
So you depend on him more and more,
Frightened of what could be in store.

He's controlling and demanding,
He needs to know all that you do,
He acts as if you are his slave,
Now, is that how boyfriends behave?

I pray my dear, you do wake up,
And tell this guy you want to break up,
Trust me, because you know it's true,
This guy really isn't good for you!

FIRST KILL

Blood stabbed,
Through sacred heart,
Aspiring psychopath,
This is his start,
Ripping at a virgins chest,
Making an awful mess,
With a mythomania tongue,
He will cover his tracks,
Stalking the shadows black,
A hollow hole that used to be his soul,
Now void within his body lies,
Vengeance and hate has consumed his being,
No longer human can he be described,
He watches her mortality slip away,
As excitement courses through his veins,
He sees the darkness come in her eyes,
Wide open with fear and surprise,
Like paint upon a canvass,
Her blood splashes acrossed his face,
Perverse enjoyment as he gets a taste,
Savouring the essence of life,
Her broken body, that once did fight,
Now lay inanimate, without life,
Ripped breast, torn flesh,
Her naked limp body now laid to rest,
The grotesque evil man has fulfilled his plan,
He apathetically throws her aside,
His cold blooded heart is satisfied,
For now......

Junkie thief

He stalks the streets in the middle of the night,
Looking for a place that's dark, without lights,
Searching for somewhere to pillage and plunder,
Out from the rock he crawled from under,
He don't care if you have a little of a lot,
He just wants enough to score a hit or a rock,
He don't care who you are or what you're going
through,
While you're asleep, he'll rob you,
With his dirty, grubby fingernails,
And body so filthy it really smells,
He'll go creeping around your house,
Sneaking around as quiet as a mouse,
Rummaging in cupboards and drawers,
Carefully opening all the doors,
So they don't make a single sound,
While he prowls around,
He has no morals or remorse,
He just don't want to be caught,
He slimes around your place,
With a wicked smile upon his face,
And when his arms are full,
When there is no more he can carry,
He'll be gone.

Visionary dreams

A visionary sits and dreams of beautiful things,
Of frost that covers a field in a sheet of white,
Reflecting the bright morning light,
Melting away, to reveal a carpet of pure delight.

Of dew drops hanging on blades of grass,
Sunlight shines through then like crystal glass,
Lighting up the meadow dusted with stars.

Of clear blue water streams,
Swirling and swiveling through the stones,
Splashing and dashing the rocks it goes.

Of diamonds on a tarmac path,
Dancing beads on an oily sea,
Twinkling for you and for me.

Of leaves or red, gold and brown,
That is on the trees all around,
Shimmering and swaying in the late summer
breeze.

It may seem like it's just a dream,
That lives within imaginary realms,
But it is real and it can be found,
As Mother Nature is all around.

Reincarnation

Each one of us is a spiritual being,
Locked within a mortal frame,
Where we can experience pleasure, suffering and
pain,
Its all for the knowledge our souls will gain,
As we travel through this mortal place,
Living our lives as the human race,
Whether you are able or disabled,
A rich man living in a stately home,
Or a homeless man in a shelter,
Its just the cards that been dealt to ya,
Next time your life might be transformed,
When it comes to your time to be reborn,
So don't be disheartened or hate another race,
Next time round you might be taking their place,
Everything we do has a lesson to be learned,
Find out what it is, there is wisdom to be earned,
When you go around with so much judgment and
hate,
One day it'll come back and slap you in the face,
Karma will repay you in this life or the next,
So be kind to all people and their pets,
It may not seem like it now but trust me its true,
You will be repaid for the good that you do.

Nightmare

I retire myself to my place of slumber,
To relinquish my restless body,
To surrender myself to sleep,
But as I lay in my darkened room,
The shadows seem to haunt me,
Horror beasties come to taunt me,
To terrorize me like before,
I see something standing by the door,
I attempt to get up, I endeavor to run,
But there is nothing that can be done,
The ghastly thing is upon me,
Its grotesque evil body weighing me down,
I try to scream, I want to shout,
But I cannot make the noise come out,
Somehow I get away, although I don't know how,
I'm running through a thicket, while wolves
around me howl,
The trees are closing in on me, ripping at my
clothes,
I squeal when I feel, my warm blood start to flow,
But the monsters still chase me, so I can not go
slow,
I feel my heart thumping deep within my chest,
I'm having palpitations because of this distress,
In my mind, I hear my thoughts,
I hear my psyche scream,
Wake up woman; it's just a dream!

Rape

No stop!
I can hear the words in my head,
You touch me,
I feel you.

No stop!
I whisper under baited breath,
You force my hands above my head,
You enter me.

No stop!
I whimper with tear filled eyes,
You do not hear my cries,
You fill me.

No stop!
I shout with authority,
Clothes shredded and torn,
But you were gone.

Autumnal Eve

The brown autumn leaves,
That rustle and crunch beneath my feet.
As I walk along the lonely street,
On a cold autumnal eve.

The bare naked limbs of the trees,
Stretch out across the sky,
Like dark bony fingers,
From which ravens and crows cry.

The North wind blows the trees,
Shaking off the last of the leaves,
That dance and sway in the breeze,
As they fall downwards to earth.

The aroma of soot fills the air,
As people light coals in their lairs,
Warm and cozy, safe and sound,
From the night that comes abound.

Empty heart with tear filled eyes,
I walk the street through the night,
So cold and full of fright,
At the end of the tunnel, I feel there is no light.

I look to a star filled sky,
Vast and shinning bright,
With no clouds to shield my sight,
They fill my heart with hope.

The endless night goes on and on,
Thousands and thousands of lights that shone,
It showed me the possibility,
That within my darkness there is a light,
Waiting to shine, big and bright.

Confidence needs to build,
Strength needs to be filled,
Creativity needs to be opened up,
For me to live life to the full,
And overflow my cup.

Hostility

Blackened sky that cries blood,
Bombs that drop from up above,
Death and destruction, no sign of love,
A deep set hatred has corrupted mankind,
Perverting and decaying their minds,
No more peace can they find.

Twisted souls with bitter hearts,
Smiling faces, Hidden masks,
Thousands and thousands of innocent lives lost,
No one cares; no one counts the cost,
Cousin fighting cousin in a blood feud war,
Watching children die fuels the hostility more.

Malevolent figures stalk streets with guns in hand,
To eliminate anyone who disagrees with their plans,
They justify a massacre,
But do they not understand,
They are continuing the lies of man,
Spreading the bitterness throughout the land.

Corrupting and contaminating the sleeping minds,
Of anyone they can find,
Brainwashing with poisonous, venomous words,
But is it not time words of peace are heard?
To put a stop to the dividing lines,
For the sake of all mankind!

We are all brothers and sisters,
No matter what we believe,
It's time to stop, this trauma and grief,
We need to learn to tolerate each other,
Live side by side and love one another.

Is romance dead?

"Is romance dead?"
The woman said,
To her lover by her side,
Red rimmed eyes from the tears she'd cried.

"No" he said with a groan,
Rolled off his back and had a moan,
"I don't know what you're talking about,
You know I still make you melt!"

"That may be so"
Was her reply,
"But the romance has definitely died,
Not long ago I was your bride."

"Stop your moaning,
You know we are tied,
We've said our vows,
Till the day we die."

"But that is not enough,
Can you not see?
I need to be shown,
That you truly love me."

"But what can I do,
To show, I do love you?
To show you I care,
And will always be there."

"Make the effort,
Like you use to,
That's what I liked,
That's what I got used to."

*"All that soppy stuff,
I use to do at the start,
That was only my way,
To get to your heart."*

"But that's why I fell for you,
Do you not understand?
Without that,
Our love is dammed."

*"But I'm your man,
And I love you through and through,
I'll tell you what, tomorrow night,
We'll have a candlelit dinner for two."*

Low self esteem

As I walk you make me look to the gutter,
Afraid to look into peoples eyes,
For I am such a lowly person,
Empty and void I feel inside,
Unworthy of love and affection you tell me,
To experience pain and suffering is my destiny,

Too afraid to have aspiration,
Too afraid to look to the sky,
Too afraid to aim high,
Confidence brought down by foolish guides,
Hope and ambition has died,
I've tried and tried without success,
To lift myself from this mess,

But you remind me, that I'm a pest,
That needs to be eradicated from society,
A freak that should have never been born,
I'm branded and scored,
From a life that's tormented me,

Then someone offers me a hand,
I regain my strength and stand,
I now understand,
To change my life is in my hands,
You used your negativity to poison my mind,
Slowly destroying me over time,

I'm glad my eyes were opened to your game,
Now I know I'm not insane,
Next time you try to drag me down,
I'm going to kick you to the ground,
Its now my time to soar,
You can hold me back no more.

Into the void

Desperately wanting something inside,
To come alive,
It feels like I'm dead,
Empty inside, a black hole,
That use to be my soul,
Now gone,
Like an urn of ashes,
I'm cold and has been,
Left on the shelf to expire,
Service no longer required,
Maybe it's my time to die,
I've let my life pass me by,
Missed every opportunity that come my way,
"That's a shame" I hear you say,
I've let fear and doubt rule my days,
And terrify my darkest nights,
Oh I'm such a sight,
I even give small children a fright,
With my scowling face and bitter tongue,
Years ago I would have been hung,
That banished hole that use to be my soul,
Now filled with anger and spite,
Bitter and twisted from my life,
Scars and wounds that never heal,
A passionate love forever be sealed,
A broken life filled with hate,
Rejected by the human race,
Another day I can not face,
I feel a total disgrace.

A false love

A false love, now lost,
The veil you used to hide,
What was hidden deep inside,
Has been removed from my eyes,
You have broken my heart in two,
You knew what you were going to do,
I would hush my lips,
If the words I spoke were untrue,
But it can not be denied,
You have manipulated and lied,
Twisted and spied,
My love for you was once true,
For a had a childlike impression of you,
My naivety prevented me from seeing,
That empty banished hole,
You call a soul,
But time prevailed over what once was,
And a love that could have crossed a timeless
boundary,
Has been brought tumbling down by you!

A lady

I would like to speak correctly,
I don't mind if I have to pay,
I would just like to speak,
In a more refined way.

I want to be taught to walk tall,
By having a book upon my head,
So as I glide down the street,
I turn people's heads.

I want to go on weekend retreats,
To relax in the countryside,
Be pampered from my head to my feet,
And sip champagne by the fireside.

I aspire to be a lady,
Dressed in expensive clothes,
Who wears fine fragrances,
That tantalise the nose.

Cotton wool hills

The cotton wool hills that fill my eyes

Stark against the clear blue sky

Shadow falls across the land

A shapeless blur of an unseen hand

Woven together with shades of green

A collage of shrubbery vast and clean

A ribbon of silvery blue, cuts through the hills

Collecting the tears the sky does spill

The muffled cries of the birds so high

As pigmented dots, against the azure sky.

Past Demons

Past demons that stalk my mind,

Past transgressions they do find,

To trip me up and make me blind,

I run away and hide,

Future is contaminated before its starts,

The demons always have the last laugh,

I try to block out the pain,

But it rebounds to pierce me again,

A thorn in my side, that will never die,

I wish the demons would say good bye!

End Poem

So there were my poems,

I hope you did enjoy,

Whether you are a girl or a boy,

There were a few crazy ones,

From the dark place in my mind,

Where poems of rape and murder you can find,

Then there are some pleasant ones,

To put a smile upon your face,

Then a few spiritual ones,

To help escape this rat race,

But ultimately, I hope you do agree,

They are all about life,

That's rich and full of diversity.

www.ingramcontent.com/pod-product-compliance
Lightning Source LLC
Chambersburg PA
CBHW060143050426
42448CB00010B/2272